The Emotionally Healthy
Woman

WORKBOOK

Resources by Pete and/or Geri Scazzero

Emotionally Healthy Spirituality (book)

Emotionally Healthy Spirituality Course (workbook and DVD)

Emotionally Healthy Spirituality Church-Wide Initiative

Emotionally Healthy Spirituality Day by Day

The Emotionally Healthy Church

The Emotionally Healthy Woman (book, workbook, and DVD)

The Emotionally Healthy Leader (coming spring 2015)

The Emotionally Healthy
Woman

EIGHT THINGS YOU HAVE *to* QUIT *to* CHANGE YOUR LIFE

Geri Scazzero
with Peter Scazzero

ZONDERVAN

The Emotionally Healthy Woman Workbook
Copyright © 2013, 2014 by Geri Scazzero and Peter L. Scazzero

This title is also available as a Zondervan ebook. Visit www.zondervan.com/ebooks.

Requests for information should be addressed to:

Zondervan, 3900 Sparks Dr. SE, Grand Rapids, Michigan 49546

ISBN 978-0-310-82822-8

Cover photo: Veer® / Ocean Photography
Author photos: Orlando Suazo
Interior illustration: 123RF® / © chatcameraman
Interior design: Beth Shagene

First Printing May 2014 / Printed in the United States of America

Contents

Contents

About the Authors

Geri Scazzero is the cofounder of New Life Fellowship Church in Queens, New York, where she serves on staff as a trainer in marriage and spiritual formation. Geri is also a popular conference speaker for church leaders, married couples, and women's groups, both in North America and internationally. She is the author of *The Emotionally Healthy Woman* and *The Emotionally Healthy Woman Workbook/DVD* and coauthor of the bestselling *Emotionally Healthy Spirituality Course* and *The Emotionally Healthy Skills 2.0* curriculum. Connect with Geri on Facebook (www.facebook.com/GeriScazzero).

Pete Scazzero is the founder of New Life Fellowship Church in Queens, New York, a large, multiracial church with more than seventy-three countries represented. After serving as senior pastor for twenty-six years, Pete now serves as a teaching pastor/pastor at large. He is the author of two bestselling books — *The Emotionally Healthy Church* and *Emotionally Healthy Spirituality*. He is also the author of *The EHS Course* and *Emotionally Healthy Spirituality Day by Day*.

Pete and Geri are the founders of Emotionally Healthy Spirituality, a groundbreaking ministry that equips churches in a deep, beneath-the-surface spiritual formation paradigm that integrates emotional health and contemplative spirituality. They have four lovely daughters. For more information, visit emotionallyhealthy.org or connect with Pete on Facebook or Twitter @petescazzero.

A Note from Geri

Dear Friend,

As I speak with women from different parts of the world, they routinely share the same struggles:

- Guilt and confusion about what it means to be a godly woman
- Exasperation with the expectations of their families and cultures
- Fear of "rocking the boat" or upsetting people
- Dissatisfaction with their marriages and relationships
- Powerlessness in the face of painful circumstances
- Sadness regarding a future that promises to be more of the same

However, I also hear a deep yearning for the freedom to blossom in their love for God, self, and others.

The *Emotionally Healthy Woman* was birthed out of my long personal journey to identify and quit behaviors that, while socially acceptable in the church, are lethal to the soul. These habits do not belong to Christ's kingdom. The "quits," the choice to do something different, emerged over a fifteen-year period. Each one was very hard-won, but in time they transformed me, my marriage, my parenting skills, our church, and many others around the world.

Choosing to do something different is not just a one-time decision; it is a lifestyle change that requires the grace and courage to quit certain unconscious ways of living. I remain more convinced than ever that the solution rests with rediscovering biblical truths that have been misconstrued or neglected.

Transformation requires intentionality, prayer, and a healthy community. My desire is that these studies and resources will provide that structure for you. *The Emotionally Healthy Woman* addresses a large, and often missing, component of our spiritual formation and discipleship today — the integration of emotional health and spiritual maturity.

Each session addresses one of the eight "quits." Each one can stand alone, but together they are a formidable force for change in your life.

Your discussions around *The Emotionally Healthy Woman* and the eight "quits" will go beyond a "tip of the iceberg" spirituality and into the depths of your being. My prayer is that, as you courageously open up that space to Jesus Christ, the Holy Spirit will enable you to experience the liberating process of receiving God's love more profoundly and becoming that love for others.

Blessings to you,
Geri

Suggested Guidelines
for the Group

Observe Confidentiality

In order to create an environment that is safe for open and honest participation, please limit your sharing to your own personal experiences. In addition, anything personal shared within the group should not be repeated outside of the group.

Speak for Yourself

Use "I" statements as often as possible.

Respect Others

Be brief in your sharing, remaining mindful that there are time limitations and others may want to share.

Turn to Wonder

If you feel judgmental or defensive when someone else is sharing, ask yourself: *I wonder what brought her to this belief? I wonder what she is feeling right now? I wonder what my reaction teaches me about myself?*

Punctuality

Resolve to begin on time and end on time, being sensitive to women with childcare or work scheduling concerns. (Sessions range from 80 – 90 minutes, though Session 1 is 95 minutes.)

Be Prepared

To get the most out of your time together, we highly recommend that you do the between-sessions reading. Please also bring your workbook with you each week.

Silence

It is okay to have silence between responses as the group shares, giving members the opportunity to reflect. Remember, there is no pressure to share.

Quit Being Afraid
of What Others Think

Introduction (1 minute)

We are so glad that you have decided to be a part of this group. We will be exploring themes that are rarely talked about in most Christian discipleship settings but which significantly impact our ability to love God, ourselves, and others well.

The following questions touch on some of the topics covered in this study and will give you an idea of the journey you are about to embark on in becoming a more *emotionally healthy woman*:

- Do you need the approval of others to feel good about yourself?
- When you are angry, sad, or disappointed, do you feel guilty about it?
- Do you believe you don't have choices?
- Do you do for others what they can and should be doing for themselves?
- Do you rarely consider your own hopes and dreams because you are so focused on others?
- Do you say *yes* when you would rather say *no*?
- Do you have difficulty speaking up when you disagree or would prefer something different?
- Are you becoming a *less* loving instead of a *more* loving person?
- Are you resentful and tired because you regularly try to do it all?
- Are you afraid to admit your weaknesses and flaws?
- Do you make assumptions (about people and situations) instead of pursuing the truth?

Growing Connected (19 minutes)

1. Share your name, what you hope to gain from this study, and a few words about something that makes you feel fully alive.

2. Have someone read aloud the "Suggested Guidelines for the Group" found right before Session 1.

VIDEO: Quit Being Afraid of What Others Think
(17 minutes)

Watch the main video segment for Session 1. Use the space provided to note anything that stands out to you.

NOTES

LARGE GROUP: Discussion (30 minutes)

Starters (10 minutes)

Turn to another person and share the following:

3. What part(s) of the video most impacted you?

4. Describe a recent situation when you either avoided saying what you *really* thought or felt, or said *yes* when you really wanted to say *no*.

Bible Study: Exodus 32:1 – 8; 19 – 21 (20 minutes)

Have a volunteer(s) read the introductory paragraph and Scripture passage, and then discuss the questions that follow.

God had already miraculously delivered the Israelites from their slavery in Egypt, but on their journey through the desert, they become nervous when Moses, their leader, was gone for forty days and nights. Upset and desperate, they sought reassurance from Aaron. Read Exodus 32:1 – 8, 19 – 21:

> [1] When the people saw that Moses was so long in coming down from the mountain, they gathered around Aaron and said, "Come, make us gods who will go before us. As for this fellow Moses who brought us up out of Egypt, we don't know what has happened to him."
> [2] Aaron answered them, "Take off the gold earrings that your wives, your sons and your daughters are wearing, and bring them to me." [3] So all the people took off their earrings and brought them to Aaron. [4] He took what they handed him and made it into an idol cast in the shape of a calf, fashioning it with a tool. Then they said, "These are your gods, Israel, who brought you up out of Egypt."
> [5] When Aaron saw this, he built an altar in front of the calf and announced, "Tomorrow there will be a festival to the LORD." [6] So the next day the people rose early and sacrificed burnt offerings and presented fellowship offerings. Afterward they sat down to eat and drink and got up to indulge in revelry.
> [7] Then the LORD said to Moses, "Go down, because your people, whom you brought up out of Egypt, have become corrupt. [8] They have been quick to turn away from what I commanded them and have

made themselves an idol cast in the shape of a calf. They have bowed down to it and sacrificed to it and have said, 'These are your gods, Israel, who brought you up out of Egypt.'"

[19] When Moses approached the camp and saw the calf and the dancing, his anger burned and he threw the tablets out of his hands, breaking them to pieces at the foot of the mountain. [20] And he took the calf the people had made and burned it in the fire; then he ground it to powder, scattered it on the water and made the Israelites drink it.

[21] He said to Aaron, "What did these people do to you, that you led them into such great sin?"

5. Imagine yourself in the scene described in verses 1 – 6. What do you see, hear, and feel?

6. As the sense of anxiety grows among the people during Moses' long absence, with whom do you most identify?

7. Aaron participated in building the golden calf because of the pressure he felt from the Israelites (see vv. 1, 23). What were the consequences of Aaron fearing what other people would think instead of listening to the voice of God (vv. 6 – 8)?

8. How might Aaron's response have been different if he had not been afraid of what others thought but had instead remained deep and secure in the love of God?

SMALL GROUP: Application (20 minutes)

Form groups of three or four for this application section. Begin by having a volunteer read the following paragraph.

Our lovability — our sense of being good enough — must come from two foundational realities: First, we are infinitely precious and valuable as image bearers of God. Second, Jesus gave up his life for each one of us. Because of these two truths, we don't have to look to any other source for our lovability.

9. Take two minutes on your own to reflect on the statements below. Place a check mark next to any statement with which you identify.

It overly affects my sense of self-worth when ...
- [ ] I don't have the approval of certain people.
- [ ] I make mistakes or fail.
- [ ] Others criticize me.
- [ ] I don't know more than others.
- [ ] I feel rejected by others.
- [ ] I don't feel needed by others.
- [ ] Others don't see me as responsible, loyal, and dependable.
- [ ] Others don't see me as special and unique.

☐ Others perceive me as weak.
☐ I'm in conflict with anyone.
☐ People are mad at me.
☐ I'm not being productive.
☐ My kids are not well behaved.
☐ People don't think well of me.
☐ Other (fill in the blank) _____

_____.

Now, briefly share your responses with your group.

10. Think over the past week. Can you recall a situation in which your response to someone was rooted more in fear than honesty? (For example, you remained silent, avoided a difficult topic, gave the impression you agreed when you didn't, or lied.)

11. The next time you find yourself in a similar situation, what can you do to slow yourself down and respond thoughtfully and truthfully?

If time allows, briefly pray for one another. Then gather again as a large group.

VIDEO: Frequently Asked Questions (5 minutes)

Watch the Frequently Asked Questions video segment for Session 1. The questions are repeated below, should you want to revisit them later on your own or with a friend or other group member. There is also some space provided for note-taking.

- In some ways, it seems like "to quit being afraid of what others think" could seem cold and unloving. Can you respond to that?
- So much of my life revolves around pleasing other people. How do I get the love of God deep into the center of my being — so that I am free to live out of God's love?

NOTES

Personal Reflection (2 minutes)

Take one minute to still your mind and heart before the Lord and respond to the following question:

What is one thing you learned about God, yourself, or others during this session? Write it down.

Spend one minute answering the following question:

What is one step you can take to quit being afraid of what others think? Write it down.

Closing Prayer (1 minute)

Use the following prayer or briefly offer your own closing prayer.

Lord, help us to quit living for the approval of others. Grant that we may rest in the freedom and joy that comes from remaining anchored in your love.

Between-Sessions Reading

Before your next meeting, read chapters 1 – 2 ("Quit Being Afraid of What Others Think" and "Quit Lying") of the book *The Emotionally Healthy Woman*.

SESSION 2

Quit Lying

✳

(90 MINUTES)

Introduction (1 minute)

It is so deeply ingrained in us to lie and live with pretense that we rarely notice when we are doing it. And if we *are* aware, we think nothing of it because we assume everyone else is doing it too. So much of our world — politics, business, paying taxes, job applications, advertising, relationships, work, and school — is shrouded in deception. We shouldn't be surprised when our churches are not the exception.

From the beginning, part of God's beautiful plan has been for human beings to live in truth. This remains central to his design for our freedom and joy. Jesus said, "If you hold to my teaching, you are really my disciples. Then you will know the truth, and the truth will set you free" (John 8:31 – 32).

As followers of Jesus Christ, the degree to which we live in truth is the degree to which we are free. When we lie in any area of our life, we shackle and chain ourselves, restricting our experience of the freedom Christ won for us.

Growing Connected (10 minutes)

Read the following verses aloud, either together or using volunteers.

> "Lord, who may dwell in your sacred tent?
>   Who may live on your holy mountain?
> The one whose walk is blameless,
>   who does what is righteous,
>   who speaks the truth from their heart" (Psalm 15:1 – 2).

> "You love evil rather than good,
>   falsehood rather than speaking the truth" (Psalm 52:3).

> "Do not lie to each other, since you have taken off your old self with its practices" (Colossians 3:9).

1. In what kinds of situations or circumstances do you find it hard to be truthful? Why?

VIDEO: Quit Lying (8 minutes)

Watch the main video segment for Session 2. Use the space provided to note anything that stands out to you.

NOTES

LARGE GROUP: Discussion (30 minutes)

Starters (10 minutes)

2. The following list includes some examples of when you might say or do something that is not completely true to what you really think or feel. Take turns reading them aloud as a group. Place a check mark next to the ones that you most relate to.

   ☐ You say *yes* when you want to say *no*.

   ☐ You smile and appear warm and friendly to someone, but you are filled with resentment toward him or her.

   ☐ You say, "We're doing just fine in our marriage," but your relationship can best be described as icy and cold.

   ☐ You say, "I'm great!" when you are not.

   ☐ You remain silent during a difficult conversation, giving the impression that you agree with what is being said. In reality, you strongly disagree.

   ☐ You say, "Sure, I'd be glad to do that for you," when you don't mean it.

   ☐ You say, "I think you did a great job," but you actually think the person's performance was adequate at best.

   ☐ You tell someone, "I don't mind that you were an hour late for our meeting," when you were actually quite annoyed.

   ☐ You give someone a hug when you don't want to.

   ☐ You lie on your tax return — or you don't pay your taxes.

   ☐ You don't say anything when a cashier mistakenly undercharges you.

3. Turn to another person and share whatever most impacted you from that exercise.

Bible Study: Acts 5:1 – 11 (20 minutes)

Have a volunteer(s) read the Acts 5:1 – 11 passage below and then answer the questions that follow.

> [1] Now a man named Ananias, together with his wife Sapphira, also sold a piece of property. [2] With his wife's full knowledge he kept back part of the money for himself, but brought the rest and put it at the apostles' feet.
>
> [3] Then Peter said, "Ananias, how is it that Satan has so filled your heart that you have lied to the Holy Spirit and have kept for yourself some of the money you received for the land? [4] Didn't it belong to you before it was sold? And after it was sold, wasn't the money at your disposal? What made you think of doing such a thing? You have not lied just to human beings but to God."
>
> [5] When Ananias heard this, he fell down and died. And great fear seized all who heard what had happened. [6] Then some young men came forward, wrapped up his body, and carried him out and buried him.
>
> [7] About three hours later his wife came in, not knowing what had happened. [8] Peter asked her, "Tell me, is this the price you and Ananias got for the land?"
>
> "Yes," she said, "that is the price."
>
> [9] Peter said to her, "How could you conspire to test the Spirit of the Lord? Listen! The feet of the men who buried your husband are at the door, and they will carry you out also."
>
> [10] At that moment she fell down at his feet and died. Then the young men came in and, finding her dead, carried her out and buried her beside her husband. [11] Great fear seized the whole church and all who heard about these events.

4. Imagine yourself witnessing the events described in the Scripture text you just read. What most shocks or surprises you?

5. Consider the difference between two offerings — the one given by Barnabas (see Acts 4:36 – 37), and the one from Ananias and Sapphira. Outwardly, both present money that they gained from the sale of property. Why do you think God intervened through Peter in such a dramatic fashion in response to Ananias and Sapphira's dishonesty?

How might the life of the church have unfolded differently had God not intervened?

6. Imagine a church, small group, workplace, or family in which people make themselves out to be more than they really are. What might be some of the implications or consequences of this?

SMALL GROUP: Application (30 minutes)

Form groups of three or four for this application section. Begin by having a volunteer or two read the following paragraphs.

One reason we lie is because we haven't learned how to speak the truth in difficult or awkward situations. Few of us have observed emotionally healthy communication modeled in our families or cultures. Yet learning these skills is crucial for spiritual maturity. Healthy communication is marked by four qualities; it is *respectful, honest, clear,* and *timely.*

Respectful: Think before you speak. Carefully describe what you want to say. Be polite, not insulting. Take the other person's feelings into account.

> Disrespectful: "That idea stinks!"
>
> Respectful: "That is an interesting idea, but I'm puzzled by ..."

Honest: Say what you *truly* think or feel; don't lie or fudge the truth.

> Dishonest: "My daughter loved the book you gave her!"
>
> Honest: "I completely forgot to give my daughter your gift, but I will write myself a reminder to make sure that I give it to her today. I think she will love it."
>
> Dishonest: "I can't go out to lunch with you today. I have too much work to do."
>
> Honest: "Thank you for your invitation to lunch, but I need some time to be alone this afternoon."

Clear: Don't beat around the bush or drop hints. Don't make a statement when you are really asking a question, or vice versa. Include details.

> Unclear: "Oh no! I'm down to my last pair of contact lenses."
>
> Clear: "Mom, would you please order me a new set of contact lenses?"
>
> Unclear: "I'd like you to cook dinner more often."
>
> Clear: "I would like you to cook dinner on Tuesdays and Thursdays, and to be completely responsible for all the ingredients you will need."

Timely: Pick a time that is convenient for both the speaker and the listener. Ideally, neither person should be tired, distracted, or tense.

> Untimely: Your husband comes home from a hard day at work, disappointed about his performance review. You begin to complain about how messy his home workspace is.

> Timely: You realize that your husband is tense and tired after a hard day at work. You wisely decide to wait for a better time (when he is relaxed) to talk with him about his workspace.

7. Recall a situation in the last few days when your speech has *not* been respectful, honest, clear, or timely. Using someone in your group as a stand-in, practice redoing that conversation — this time speaking respectfully, honestly, and clearly, and considering whether you were timely in your original approach.

8. We often internalize unspoken messages from our families and culture that make it easy for us to lie to ourselves or to others. What is one message you unconsciously internalized growing up that impacts your ability to be truthful? (For example: Don't show your feelings. Don't talk back. Always be nice. Don't fight. Always be good. You must be successful. Always be on time. Mistakes can kill, so never make one — and never admit to making one.)

9. The following quotation, from Thomas Merton's *New Seeds of Contemplation*, addresses the choice God has given each of us to be truthful or dishonest. Read it as a group.

> Trees and animals have no problem. God makes them what they are without consulting them, and they are perfectly satisfied. With

us it is different. God leaves us free to be whatever we like. We can be ourselves or not, as we please. We are at liberty to be real, or to be unreal. We may be true or false, the choice is ours. We may wear now one mask and now another, and never, if we so desire, appear with our own true face.[1]

In what situations (or with whom) are you most tempted to wear a mask and not "appear with [your] own true face"?

If time allows, briefly pray for one another. Then gather again as a large group.

VIDEO: Frequently Asked Questions (8 minutes)

Watch the Frequently Asked Questions video segment for Session 2. The questions are repeated below, should you want to revisit them later on your own or with a friend or other group member. There is also some space provided for note-taking.

- If I start being truthful with the people around me, there will be a lot of conflict. I hate conflict. What advice do you have for me?
- It seems like being truthful in all situations could really hurt some people. Are there ever times when it is better to withhold certain truths, yet not cross the line into lying?

NOTES

Personal Reflection (2 minutes)

Take one minute to still your mind and heart before the Lord and respond to the following question:

> *What is one thing you learned about God, yourself, or others during this session? Write it down.*

Spend one minute answering the following question:

> *What is one step you can take this week to consciously speak accurately and truthfully? Write it down.*

Closing Prayer (1 minute)

Use the following prayer or offer your own closing prayer.

Lord, help us to see where we don't live in truth, as well as the consequences of that dishonesty for us and our relationships. Fill us with the Holy Spirit, who is called the Spirit of truth in John 16:13. Thank you for the safety net of your love. In Jesus' name, amen.

Between-Sessions Reading

Before your next meeting, read chapter 3 ("Quit Dying to the Wrong Things") of the book *The Emotionally Healthy Woman*.

Quit Dying to
the Wrong Things

✳

(85 MINUTES)

Introduction (1 minute)

Jesus calls us to take up our cross and follow him. However, it is essential, for the sakes of our souls, to distinguish between what we should and should not die to. For example, God calls us to die to selfishness, but he *does not* call us to die to self-care.

When we die to the wrong things, we often grow tired, frustrated, and resentful. We wonder what went wrong.

When we delight in the good gifts and pleasures God provides for us, we come alive for him, ourselves, and others. In fact, making space in life for delight is an important part of being a follower of Jesus. Failing to do so is a tragic misapplication of what it means to lay down our lives for Christ.

Growing Connected (10 minutes)

1. Turn to another person in the group and answer the following question: What is one thing that brought you sheer delight this past week?

VIDEO: Quit Dying to the Wrong Things (8 minutes)

Watch the main video segment for Session 3. Use the space provided to note anything that stands out to you.

NOTES

LARGE GROUP: **Discussion** (30 minutes)

Starters (10 minutes)

2. Self-care is never selfish. It includes things such as saying a healthy no, being with people you enjoy, doing things that make you feel alive, getting enough sleep, and eating well. What obstacles or hindrances keep you from healthy self-care?

Bible Study: Genesis 1:1 – 4, 10, 12, 16 – 18, 21, 25 – 26, 31
(20 minutes)

Have a volunteer(s) read the selected verses below from Genesis 1 and then answer the questions that follow.

[1] In the beginning God created the heavens and the earth. [2] Now the earth was formless and empty, darkness was over the surface of the deep, and the Spirit of God was hovering over the waters.

[3] And God said, "Let there be light," and there was light. [4] God saw that the light was good, and he separated the light from the darkness.

[10] God called the dry ground "land," and the gathered waters he called "seas." And God saw that it was good.

[12] The land produced vegetation: plants bearing seed according to their kinds and trees bearing fruit with seed in it according to their kinds. And God saw that it was good.

[16] God made two great lights — the greater light to govern the day and the lesser light to govern the night. He also made the stars. [17] God set them in the vault of the sky to give light on the earth, [18] to govern the day and the night, and to separate light from darkness. And God saw that it was good.

[21] So God created the great creatures of the sea and every living thing with which the water teems and that moves about in it,

according to their kinds, and every winged bird according to its kind. And God saw that it was good.

[25] God made the wild animals according to their kinds, the livestock according to their kinds, and all the creatures that move along the ground according to their kinds. And God saw that it was good.

[26] Then God said, "Let us make mankind in our image, in our likeness, so that they may rule over the fish in the sea and the birds in the sky, over the livestock and all the wild animals, and over all the creatures that move along the ground."

[31] God saw all that he had made, and it was very good. And there was evening, and there was morning—the sixth day.

3. Genesis 1 gives a lovely picture of God's creation of the world and how he felt about it. How does the repeated phrase "it was good" speak to you?

4. It is easy to go through life and not see or enjoy God's gifts. How have you joined God in delighting in the world he has created (e.g., by enjoying food, beauty, nature, people, music, or art)?

In what other ways would you like to join him?

5. Scripture teaches that we, as human beings, are both good (Genesis 1 – 2) *and* sinners (Genesis 3). What are the dangers of overemphasizing one or the other — our good or sinful natures?

6. Spiritual formation author Henri Nouwen wrote these words:

> For a very long time I considered low self-esteem to be some kind of virtue. I had been warned so often against pride and conceit that I came to consider it a good thing to deprecate myself. But now I realize that the real sin is to deny God's first love for me, to ignore my original goodness. Because without claiming that first love and that original goodness for myself, I lose touch with my true self and embark on the destructive search among the wrong people and in the wrong places for what can only be found in the house of my Father.[2]

What words or phrases call out to you from this quotation? Why?

SMALL GROUP: Application (26 minutes)

Form groups of three or four for this application section. Complete question 7 on your own and then discuss questions 8 – 10 in your small group.

7. In order to quit dying to the wrong things, we first need to be aware of what nurtures our spirit and brings us delight. In the space below, take no more than five minutes to make a personal list of everything you like to do — everything that fills you with delight. Your list might include gardening, walking the dog, being out in nature, spending time with or talking to close friends, cooking, painting, certain spiritual practices, or visiting particular places — *anything* that you find life-giving. Don't hold back. List everything that comes to mind.

   My spirit is nurtured by the following:

8. Share what the experience of making your list was like for you.

9. What is one thing from your list that you want to integrate, or integrate more deeply, into your life right away? What adjustments might you need to make for this to happen?

10. Share one or two things you need to die to. (For example: judgmental attitude, envy, defensiveness, perfectionism, lying.)

If time allows, briefly pray for one another. Then gather again as a large group.

VIDEO: Frequently Asked Questions (7 minutes)

Watch the Frequently Asked Questions video segment for Session 3. The questions are repeated below, should you want to revisit them later on your own or with a friend or other group member. There is also some space provided for note-taking.

- What is the difference between self-care and selfishness?
- How do I develop my God-given self or nurture my true self?

NOTES

Personal Reflection (2 minutes)

Take one minute to still your mind and heart before the Lord and respond to the following question:

> *What is one thing you learned about God, yourself, or others during this session? Write it down.*

Spend one minute answering the following question:

> *What is one step you can take to quit dying to the wrong things? Write it down.*

Closing Prayer (1 minute)

Use the following prayer or briefly offer your own closing prayer.

Lord, help us to remember that we are made by you — invaluable, unrepeatable, and unique. Teach us also to delight in the many gifts you have placed in and around each of us. Shine a light on the sinful areas of our lives that you want to change. In Jesus' name, amen.

Between-Sessions Reading

Before your next meeting, read chapter 4 ("Quit Denying Anger, Sadness, and Fear") of the book *The Emotionally Healthy Woman*.

Quit Denying Anger, Sadness, and Fear

✿

(90 MINUTES)

Introduction (1 minute)

The Psalms have remained the most popular book of the Bible for centuries. These 150 songs express the entire range of human emotions with unashamed and uninhibited freedom. We observe David (among others) pouring out the full intensity of his raw emotions before the Lord. He does not hide behind a spiritual veneer of "being good." He does not pretend everything is fine when it is not. He does not suppress, deny, or minimize what is going on inside of him.

Many of us, however, have an unbiblical, inhuman, and muddled relationship with our emotions — especially anger, sadness, and fear. But as we shall see, God wants *all* of our emotions to be our teachers — to shape and mature us into godly women who hear his voice, know the depths of who we are, and love others well.

Growing Connected (10 minutes)

1. On your own, complete the following assessment[3] as honestly as possible. Use this scoring method: 1 – very rarely true, 2 – sometimes true, 3 – often true, 4 – very often true.

It's easy for me to identify what I am feeling inside.   1　2　3　4

I am able to experience and express my anger in a way that leads to growth in others and myself.   1　2　3　4

I am honest with myself (and with those I trust) about my fears and doubts.   1　2　3　4

When I go through a disappointment or a loss, I reflect on how I'm feeling. I don't pretend that nothing is wrong.   1　2　3　4

I am able to cry, experience my depression or sadness, explore the reasons behind it, and allow God to work in me through it.   1　2　3　4

Now, briefly share with the group one thing you learned about yourself while taking this inventory.

VIDEO: Quit Denying Anger, Sadness, and Fear
(11 minutes)

Watch the main video segment for Session 4. Use the space provided to note anything that stands out to you.

NOTES

LARGE GROUP: Discussion (35 minutes)

Starters (10 minutes)

2. Take a few minutes to respond to each of the following prompts in the space provided; then find a partner and share your answers with each other.

   What did the family you grew up in teach you about dealing with the following emotions?

   Anger (e.g., stuff it, explode, only certain people can get angry)

   Sadness (e.g., get over it, crying is a sign of weakness, sadness is selfish)

   Fear (e.g., ignore it, deny it, be paralyzed by it)

Bible Study: Psalm 22:1 – 2, 7 – 14 (25 minutes)

Have a volunteer(s) read the selected verses below from Psalm 22 and then discuss the questions that follow.

> [1] My God, my God, why have you forsaken me?
>   Why are you so far from saving me,
>   so far from my cries of anguish?

² My God, I cry out by day, but you do not answer,
  by night, but I find no rest.
⁷ All who see me mock me;
  they hurl insults, shaking their heads.
⁸ "He trusts in the LORD," they say,
  "let the LORD rescue him.
Let him deliver him,
  since he delights in him."
⁹ Yet you brought me out of the womb;
  you made me trust in you, even at my mother's breast.
¹⁰ From birth I was cast on you;
  from my mother's womb you have been my God.
¹¹ Do not be far from me,
  for trouble is near
  and there is no one to help.
¹² Many bulls surround me;
  strong bulls of Bashan encircle me.
¹³ Roaring lions that tear their prey
  open their mouths wide against me.
¹⁴ I am poured out like water,
  and all my bones are out of joint.
My heart has turned to wax;
  it has melted within me.

3. David, the writer of Psalm 22, is well known for being a man after God's own heart. How does he describe his emotional life before God in these verses? Be specific.

4. The depth of David's grief and sadness is clearly evident in this passage. How does this compare to the widely accepted (and often not-so-subtle) message that "good" Christians aren't supposed to feel hurt, confused, or discouraged?

5. It has been said that anger is often a surface or "secondary" feeling. It often grows out of another emotion that exists deeper beneath the surface — such as sadness, fear, or shame. Does this idea ring true with you? Can you think of an example from your own life?

6. When you consider David's example of not denying or ignoring anger, sadness, or fear, what resonates with you?

SMALL GROUP: Application (25 minutes)

Form groups of three or four for the application section.

7. Think of a recent experience that caused a physical reaction in your body — a tightening in your chest, a knot in your stomach, a stress headache, the grinding of your teeth, the clenching of your hands, sweaty palms, tension in your shoulders, the tapping of your foot, or insomnia. What could your body have been trying to tell you about what was going on inside of you?

8. There are three steps to help you quit denying your anger, sadness, and fear:

   • Feel your feelings.
   • Think through your feelings. Ask yourself: *What are the reasons I am feeling this way?*
   • Take appropriate action.

   Which of these three steps do you most need to focus on in your spiritual journey right now? Explain.

9. One of the central messages of Christianity is that suffering and death eventually lead to resurrection and new life. What gifts of new life from God might be waiting to emerge once you embrace your anger, sadness, and fear?

   If time allows, briefly pray for one another. Then gather again as a large group.

VIDEO: Frequently Asked Questions (5 minutes)

Watch the Frequently Asked Questions video segment for Session 4. The questions are repeated below, should you want to revisit them later on your own or with a friend or other group member. There is also some space provided for note-taking.

- It seems like you are saying to follow my feelings — and not Jesus or Scripture. I have a friend who says that if you open up this Pandora's box, there is no closing it. What would you say to her?

- I am afraid to let myself feel all of my emotions, especially my anger. I am fearful that I will hurt people and wander from God's intention that I be a loving person. How do I keep that from happening?

NOTES

Personal Reflection (2 minutes)

Take one minute to still your mind and heart before the Lord and respond to the following question:

What is one thing you learned about God, yourself, or others during this session? Write it down.

Spend one minute answering the following question:

What is one step you can take to quit denying your anger, sadness, and fear? Write it down.

Closing Prayer (1 minute)

Use the following prayer or briefly offer your own closing prayer.

Lord, we bring to you all of our feelings of anger, sadness, and fear. Show us how to embrace our full humanity as Jesus did, and help us to be attentive to what you are doing in the midst of our "difficult" emotions.

Between-Sessions Reading

Before your next meeting, read chapter 5 ("Quit Blaming") of the book *The Emotionally Healthy Woman.*

SESSION 5

Quit Blaming

✻

(80 MINUTES)

Introduction (1 minute)

When things don't go our way, we blame our parents, spouse, children, boss, friends, leaders, or coworkers. We blame demonic powers or even God himself when things are *really* bad.

Blaming comforts us, at least for a while, with the illusion that we are in control. However, it actually accomplishes the opposite, stripping us of our God-given individual power and keeping us helplessly stuck in immaturity.

As human beings created in God's image, we are born with certain rights and responsibilities that enable us to walk in our God-given personal freedom (Genesis 1:26 – 31). We can make choices, set boundaries, say no, declare our preferences, and think for ourselves.

When we quit blaming and instead utilize our God-given personal freedom, our sense of helplessness evaporates. We realize that other people are not responsible for our happiness. We are. We can't change others, but we *can* change ourselves — with God's grace.

Growing Connected (5 minutes)

1. Turn to someone else in the group and share an example of a time when you felt unfairly blamed for something (e.g., by your spouse, friend, child, boss, coworker, or parent). How did that experience make you feel?

VIDEO: Quit Blaming (9 minutes)

Watch the main video segment for Session 5. Use the space provided to note anything that stands out to you.

NOTES

LARGE GROUP: Discussion (30 minutes)

Starters (10 minutes)

2. Have a group member read aloud the following examples of blaming:

- My boss makes my life miserable.
- I'm exhausted because my spouse won't agree to take a vacation.
- I'm in debt because my job doesn't pay enough.
- My marriage is hard because my husband won't go to counseling.
- I'm a single mom; I will struggle for the rest of my life.
- My parents are ruining my life.
- I'm overweight because I have no time to go to the gym.
- My life is hard because my kids won't listen to me.

Think of a recent time when you were angry. Who (or what) were you tempted to blame? Share your answer with the group.

Bible Study: Genesis 3:6 – 13 (20 minutes)

Have a volunteer(s) read the introductory paragraph and Scripture passage, and then discuss the questions that follow.

Adam and Eve experienced perfect communion with God and with one another. However, after they turned away from God, their relationship dramatically changed, as Genesis 3:6 – 13 describes:

> [6] When the woman saw that the fruit of the tree was good for food and pleasing to the eye, and also desirable for gaining wisdom, she took some and ate it. She also gave some to her husband, who was with her, and he ate it. [7] Then the eyes of both of them were opened, and they realized they were naked; so they sewed fig leaves together and made coverings for themselves.
>
> [8] Then the man and his wife heard the sound of the LORD God as he was walking in the garden in the cool of the day, and they hid from the LORD God among the trees of the garden. [9] But the LORD God called to the man, "Where are you?"
>
> [10] He answered, "I heard you in the garden, and I was afraid because I was naked; so I hid."
>
> [11] And he said, "Who told you that you were naked? Have you eaten from the tree that I commanded you not to eat from?"
>
> [12] The man said, "The woman you put here with me — she gave me some fruit from the tree, and I ate it."
>
> [13] Then the LORD God said to the woman, "What is this you have done?" The woman said, "The serpent deceived me, and I ate."

3. How would you describe Adam and Eve's relationship with God in verses 8 – 13?

How would you describe their relationship with each other?

4. What feelings might be behind Adam's and Eve's blaming (vv. 12 – 13)?

5. Genesis 3 gives us a picture of how the *first* human family resorted to blaming. Describe what blaming looked like in *your* family growing up. How did that make you feel?

6. In what area(s) of your life are you most tempted to blame others? And who are you most often tempted to blame? (For example: spouse, children, parents, friends, coworkers, or authority figures.)

SMALL GROUP: Application (27 minutes)

Form groups of three or four for this application section. Begin by having a volunteer read the following paragraph (or the group leader may opt instead to offer a fuller summary from *The Emotionally Healthy Woman* book). Next, on your own, respond to the nine prompts that begin question 7. Finally, discuss your responses with your small group.

The Personal Freedom Toolkit referred to in *The Emotionally Healthy Woman*[4] reminds us of our rights and responsibilities as human beings made in God's image.[5] It equips us to assert ourselves rather than to cast blame. As author John Powell has said, "If I can only cross over the line that separates the blamers from those who accept the full responsibility for their behavior, it will probably be the most mature thing I have ever done."[6]

7. Take one minute after reading each tool and its accompanying question to write your response in the space provided.

   The Fence of Separateness: Where and when do you allow your boundaries to be crossed?

   The Voice of Declaration: When (and with whom) do you have difficulty speaking up?

   The Yes/No Medallion: To whom do you find it difficult to say no?

The Heart of Feelings: Which feelings do you avoid?

The Oxygen Mask of Self-Care: Where are you failing in self-care?

The Mirror of Self-Confrontation: Which truths about yourself are you avoiding?

The Key of Hope: In which areas of your life do you think things will never change?

The Hat of Wisdom: In which areas of your life are you being impulsive and not asking the difficult questions?

The Badge of Courage: For which one of these tools do you need the most courage?

Now, share the *two* tools that are most significant for you today and why.

If time allows, briefly pray for one another. Then gather again as a large group.

VIDEO: Frequently Asked Questions (5 minutes)

Watch the Frequently Asked Questions video segment for Session 5. The questions are repeated below, should you want to revisit them later on your own or with a friend or other group members. There is also some space provided for note-taking.

- When I think about using the Personal Freedom Toolkit, I worry that I will get a lot of resistance from those around me. It is a little overwhelming for me and seems very hard to do. Can you suggest some first steps?

- At what point does the fence of separateness become a wall that people cannot penetrate? When does it become isolating and unloving?

- I don't believe that I have any choices in my situation right now. What advice do you have for me?

NOTES

Personal Reflection (2 minutes)

Take one minute to still your mind and heart before the Lord and respond to the following question:

What is one thing you learned about God, yourself, or others during this session? Write it down.

Spend one minute answering the following question:

What is one step you can take to assume responsibility for your life and quit blaming? Write it down.

Closing Prayer (1 minute)

Use the following prayer or briefly offer your own closing prayer.

Lord, forgive us for turning away from you by blaming others. Cleanse us. Grant each of us the courage and wisdom to implement the tools needed to take responsibility for our lives. In Jesus' name, amen.

Between-Sessions Reading

Before your next meeting, read chapter 6 ("Quit Overfunctioning") of the book *The Emotionally Healthy Woman*.

SESSION 6

Quit Overfunctioning

(80 MINUTES)

Introduction (1 minute)

Overfunctioning is doing for others what they can and should be doing for themselves. Often, wherever you find an overfunctioner, there is an underfunctioner close behind.

Overfunctioning is particularly difficult to identify and remedy because we get rewarded for it, especially in the church. However, it damages friendships, marriages, churches, workplaces, and families. When we overfunction, we end up believing that if we let go, things will fall apart. Actually, the opposite is true. If we let go of our overfunctioning ways, then God's work will prosper — in us and, ultimately, in many others.

Growing Connected (9 minutes)

1. Overfunctioning exists on a continuum that ranges from mild to severe. Use the simple assessment below to get an idea of where you fall on the overfunctioning continuum. As a volunteer reads the list aloud, place a check mark next to each statement that describes you.

   ☐ I generally know the right way to do things.

   ☐ I am quick to offer advice or fix things so they don't fall apart.

   ☐ I have difficulty allowing others to struggle with their own problems.

   ☐ In the long run, it is simply easier for me to do things myself.

   ☐ I don't trust others to do as good a job as I can.

   ☐ I often do whatever is asked of me, even if I'm already overloaded.

   ☐ I don't like to rock the boat, so I cover for the shortcomings of others.

   ☐ People describe me as stable and as always having it together.

   ☐ I don't like asking for help because I don't want to be a burden.

   ☐ I like to be needed.

   If you checked two or three statements, you may be overfunctioning. If you checked four to seven, you probably have a moderate case of overfunctioning. If you checked eight or more, you are in trouble — you are a chronic overfunctioner!

2. Turn to someone else in the group and share one insight you gained from taking this assessment.

VIDEO: Quit Overfunctioning (9 minutes)

Watch the main video segment for Session 6. Use the space provided to note anything that stands out to you.

NOTES

LARGE GROUP: Discussion (30 minutes)

Starters (5 minutes)

3. Name one situation in which you are currently doing for someone else something he or she could and should be doing.

Bible Study: Luke 10:38 – 42 (25 minutes)

Have a volunteer(s) read the introductory paragraphs and Scripture passage, and then discuss the questions that follow.

In this passage, Martha is completely caught up in the demands of preparing a meal for Jesus and his twelve disciples. Among other things, her to-do list probably includes shopping for ingredients; setting a large table; preparing the food; borrowing mats, tables, and serving plates from neighbors; cleaning the house; serving the meal; and (perhaps most significantly) wanting everything to go perfectly.

Martha is attempting to accomplish too much. She becomes so caught up in the details of her work that she loses sight of the most important thing — being present with Jesus. Read Luke 10:38 – 42:

> [38] As Jesus and his disciples were on their way, he came to a village where a woman named Martha opened her home to him. [39] She had a sister called Mary, who sat at the Lord's feet listening to what he said. [40] But Martha was distracted by all the preparations that had to be made. She came to him and asked, "Lord, don't you care that my sister has left me to do the work by myself? Tell her to help me!"
>
> [41] "Martha, Martha," the Lord answered, "you are worried and upset about many things, [42] but few things are needed — or indeed only one. Mary has chosen what is better, and it will not be taken away from her."

4. What words or phrases describe Martha's inner, troubled emotional state in verses 40 – 42?

Describe her attitude toward Jesus and Mary in verse 40.

5. Put yourself in Martha's shoes. What might be driving her level of distraction and worry? (For example: she doesn't like to ask for help, needs to be in control, etc.)

6. What are some different choices Martha could have made so that she would have found the event less stressful and more enjoyable?

7. Jesus tenderly responds to Martha's anxiety by inviting her to join Mary at his feet, saying, "Martha, dear Martha, you're fussing far too much and getting yourself worked up over nothing. One thing only is essential" (Luke 10:41 – 42 MSG). Insert your name in Martha's place. How do you hear these warm words for yourself?

SMALL GROUP: Application (25 minutes)

Form groups of three or four to complete this application section.

8. Try to think of a specific situation in which you might be overfunctioning. Where is God inviting you to let go — at home, at work, at church, in a friendship, with your extended family, etc.?

What is one negative consequence of your overfunctioning? (For example: it breeds resentment, perpetuates immaturity, prevents you from focusing on your life's calling, erodes your spiritual life, destroys community.)

9. There are many different reasons *why* we overfunction. Have someone slowly read aloud the sentence stems in the "Reasons I Overfunction" column of the following table. Identify *one* reason for overfunctioning that most resonates with you and complete the sentence stem for yourself.

Reasons I Overfunction	Remedies
I don't want to ask for help because …	I can ask for help because …
I need to have things a certain way because …	I don't always need to have things my way because …
I need to be in control because …	I don't always need to be in control because …
If I let go, things will fall apart because …	I can let things go because …
My way is best because …	My way is not always the best way because …
I have to do everything myself because …	I don't have to do everything myself because …
Other:	Other:

10. Now, as a group, complete the sentence stems in the "Remedies" column of the table, slowly going down the list one by one.

If time allows, briefly pray for one another. Then gather again as a large group.

VIDEO: Frequently Asked Questions (3 minutes)

Watch the Frequently Asked Questions video segment for Session 6. The questions are repeated below, should you want to revisit them later on your own or with a friend or other group member. There is also some space provided for note-taking.

- I worry that if I attempt to quit overfunctioning, I could become selfish and *less* loving. I don't trust myself. I know many Christians who don't do anything to serve others. How do you respond to that?
- What about situations in which God *does* call us to overfunction for people (e.g., a parent with Alzheimers or a child with a disability)?
- I don't understand what you mean when you say, "Wherever there is an overfunctioner, there is usually an underfunctioner. For the underfunctioner to change, the overfunctioner must change first." When have you seen this to be true?

NOTES

Personal Reflection (2 minutes)

Take one minute to still your mind and heart before the Lord and respond to the following question:

> *What is one thing you learned about God, yourself, or others during this session? Write it down.*

Spend one minute answering the following question:

> *What is one step you can take to quit overfunctioning? Write it down.*

Closing Prayer (1 minute)

Use the following prayer or briefly offer your own closing prayer.

Lord, help us to love others well, to live faithful to our unique lives, and to honor our own boundaries and limits. Help us to trust that you are on the throne and that "your arm is not too short" to take care of the people and situations we care about. In Jesus' name, amen.

Between-Sessions Reading

Before your next meeting, read chapter 7 ("Quit Faulty Thinking") of the book *The Emotionally Healthy Woman*.

Quit Faulty
Thinking

(90 MINUTES)

Introduction (1 minute)

Faulty thinking is the act of believing something is true when it is false. As Mark Twain once said, "It isn't what you don't know that gets you into trouble; it's what you know for sure that just isn't so."

Faulty thinking is rarely talked about in our churches or addressed in spiritual formation or discipleship training. But when we choose to quit feeding these simple — but destructive — distortions, we get freed from powerlessness, hopelessness, false guilt, and unnecessary pain.

What makes faulty thinking so dangerous is that it operates, for the most part, by making assumptions beyond our conscious awareness. Moreover, it is contagious and spreads like wildfire. There are innumerable ways we engage in faulty thinking in our lives. Each one has vast consequences, affecting how we live out our faith in Jesus Christ and blocking the power of God's Spirit from flowing in and through us.

Growing Connected (9 minutes)

1. Would you describe the lens through which your parents (or primary caregivers) saw the world as a "glass half empty" or a "glass half full" mentality? How has this impacted the way you see the world?

VIDEO: Quit Faulty Thinking (10 minutes)

Watch the main video segment for Session 7. Use the space provided to note anything that stands out to you.

NOTES

LARGE GROUP: Discussion (35 minutes)

Starters (10 minutes)

2. Think of a time when someone made an assumption about you that was false. How did that impact you? (For example: My brother didn't invite me to his wife's birthday party because he assumed I was too busy to attend. This made me very sad. / My supervisor assumed that I wouldn't want to go away overnight for advanced training. I was angry and sad to have missed out on that opportunity. / My friend assumed I was being insensitive and rude when I didn't respond to her email invitation. The truth is, I never received it.)

Bible Study: 1 Kings 19:1 – 12, 18 (25 minutes)

Have a volunteer(s) read the introductory paragraph and Scripture passage, and then discuss the questions that follow.

Imagine living in a country where only a handful of Christians remain. There are no churches, no Bible studies, no opportunities for fellowship, and no Christian books. The prophet Elijah faced a similar situation. The nation of Israel had abandoned the Lord God for another god — Baal. We join Elijah's story after he has publicly defeated 450 false prophets of Baal and given witness to the power of the God of Israel (1 Kings 18). Ahab and Jezebel are the reigning king and queen of Israel. Read 1 Kings 19:1 – 12, 18:

[1] Now Ahab told Jezebel everything Elijah had done and how he had killed all the prophets with the sword. [2] So Jezebel sent a messenger to Elijah to say, "May the gods deal with me, be it ever so severely, if by this time tomorrow I do not make your life like that of one of them."

[3] Elijah was afraid and ran for his life. When he came to Beersheba in Judah, he left his servant there, [4] while he himself went a day's journey into the wilderness. He came to a broom bush, sat down under it and prayed that he might die. "I have had enough, LORD," he said. "Take my life; I am no better than my ancestors." [5] Then he lay down under the bush and fell asleep.

All at once an angel touched him and said, "Get up and eat." [6] He looked around, and there by his head was some bread baked over hot coals, and a jar of water. He ate and drank and then lay down again.

[7] The angel of the LORD came back a second time and touched him and said, "Get up and eat, for the journey is too much for you." [8] So he got up and ate and drank. Strengthened by that food, he traveled forty days and forty nights until he reached Horeb, the mountain of God. [9] There he went into a cave and spent the night.

And the word of the LORD came to him: "What are you doing here, Elijah?"

[10] He replied, "I have been very zealous for the LORD God Almighty. The Israelites have rejected your covenant, torn down your altars, and put your prophets to death with the sword. I am the only one left, and now they are trying to kill me too."

[11] The LORD said, "Go out and stand on the mountain in the presence of the LORD, for the LORD is about to pass by."

Then a great and powerful wind tore the mountains apart and shattered the rocks before the LORD, but the LORD was not in the wind. After the wind there was an earthquake, but the LORD was not in the earthquake. [12] After the earthquake came a fire, but the LORD was not in the fire. And after the fire came a gentle whisper.

[18] "Yet I [the LORD] reserve seven thousand in Israel — all whose knees have not bowed down to Baal and whose mouths have not kissed him."

3. How would you describe Elijah's emotional state when he hears of Jezebel's threat to kill him (vv. 3 – 5)?

4. After God sends an angel to feed and strengthen him, Elijah goes into a cave to spend the night. In your own words, explain Elijah's response (v. 10) to the Lord's question, "What are you doing here, Elijah?"

5. Consider the following statements that each reveal Elijah's faulty thinking:

   "Take my life; I am no better than my ancestors" (v. 4).

   "I am the only one left, and now they are trying to kill me too" (v. 10).

   How does God address Elijah's distorted thinking (vv. 5 – 7, 18)?

6. The course of Elijah's life was dramatically changed when he allowed God to correct his faulty thinking. In what situations, or with whom, might faulty assumptions be negatively impacting you today?

SMALL GROUP: Application (23 minutes)

Form groups of three or four to complete this application section. Begin by having a volunteer read the introductory paragraphs below. Work through question 7 together and question 8 on your own and together. Afterward, reconvene the large group to assess the exercise (question 9).

There are three major types of faulty thinking that distort how we see and experience life:

- *Taking Things Personally* causes us to take offense, responsibility, or the blame before we have all the facts.
- *Thinking Things Will Never Change* makes us believe that the past inevitably determines the future.
- *All-or-Nothing Thinking (Overgeneralizing)* exaggerates our circumstances and uses words like *always, all, everybody,* or *never.*

7. Together, read through the examples below and then fill in a response for the empty box in each category.

Taking Things Personally

Faulty Thinking	Accurate Thinking
The pastor said hello to my friend, but he didn't say hello to me. He must not like me.	It is possible that the pastor didn't see me, or was distracted, or didn't know I was expecting a greeting.
My boss showed up late for a meeting with me today. She must not think much of me.	My boss is often late for meetings. She may not have even realized that she was late. Perhaps something unexpected came up, or she encountered traffic and just didn't mention it to me.
My friend never responded to my email invitation for lunch. I must not be important to her.	

Thinking Things Will Never Change

Faulty Thinking	Accurate Thinking
I'll never find a good church that I like.	There are many good churches out there. It may take some patience as I search, but I will eventually find a church that I like.
My life will always be difficult because my child has a learning disability.	I can find resources that will help me better deal with my child's difficulties. The future doesn't have to be as difficult as the past has been.
I'll never be in a healthy dating relationship.	

cont.

All-or-Nothing Thinking (Overgeneralizing)

Faulty Thinking	Accurate Thinking
My car broke down again. Everything is going wrong for me!	Although my car broke down, there are a number of things that are right with my life—my health, job, family, friends, etc.
You can't trust lawyers.	It is true that there are some dishonest lawyers, but there are also lawyers who can be trusted.
My coworker is a terrible employee.	

8. In the boxes below:

   • Under "Faulty Thinking," write one faulty thought that you've had recently. (Choose from one of the three main categories outlined earlier.)
   • Under "Accurate Thinking," rewrite your faulty thought so that it reflects more accurate thinking. (If any of you become stuck, help each other with the exercise.)
   • Share your responses with the other members of your group.

Faulty Thinking	Accurate Thinking

LARGE GROUP: Exercise Assessment (5 minutes)

9. Reconvene the large group and share your answers to the following question: What did you learn from doing this exercise?

VIDEO: Frequently Asked Questions (4 minutes)

Watch the Frequently Asked Questions video segment for Session 7. The questions are repeated below, should you want to revisit them later on your own or with a friend or other group member. There is also some space provided for note-taking.

- Aren't there other types of faulty thinking — especially in the Christian life? Why did you choose just the three specific types of faulty thinking you discussed in this session?

- I'm confused. In Session 4 you told us to quit denying our anger, sadness, and fear. Yet now it seems like you are telling us to quit following our feelings. Which is it?

NOTES

Personal Reflection (2 minutes)

Take one minute to still your mind and heart before the Lord and respond to the following question:

> *What is one thing you learned about God, yourself, or others during this session? Write it down.*

Spend one minute answering the following question:

> *What is one step you can take to avoid faulty thinking? Write it down.*

Closing Prayer (1 minute)

Use the following prayer or briefly offer your own closing prayer.

Jesus, show each of us where we are engaging in faulty thinking. Help us to live in what is true, to quit making assumptions, and to not take things personally. Fill us with the Holy Spirit's power to align our thinking with the truth. In Jesus' name, amen.

Between-Sessions Reading

Before your next meeting, read chapter 8 ("Quit Living Someone Else's Life") of the book *The Emotionally Healthy Woman*.

Quit Living
Someone Else's Life

(90 MINUTES)

Introduction (1 minute)

God has made each of us unique and unrepeatable. He has deposited into each of us a distinct combination of gifts and preferences, as well as a particular temperament and personality. He has also birthed us into a precise moment in history in a specific part of the world. In doing so, God has crafted a personalized destiny for each of us.

Living our unique life, however, is easier said than done. As the renowned poet E. E. Cummings (1894 – 1962) once said, "It takes great courage to grow up and turn out to be who you really are." It takes great intentionality to faithfully live out your destiny.

Despite the great pressures and expectations placed on him by others, Jesus stayed true to his own life and purpose, finishing the work the Father had given him to do (John 17:4).

In the same way, God calls each of us to wholeheartedly pursue our God-given life and to not let the expectations of others steer us off course. In doing so, we are set free and, ultimately, those around us are set free as well.

Growing Connected (4 minutes)

1. Whom do you have difficulty disappointing? Why?

VIDEO: Quit Living Someone Else's Life (10 minutes)

Watch the main video segment for Session 8. Use the space provided to note anything that stands out to you.

NOTES

LARGE GROUP: Discussion (30 minutes)

Starters (10 minutes)

2. Turn to another person in the group and answer the following question: When (or with whom) do you feel pressured to *not* be yourself?

Bible Study: Mark 3:20 – 22, 31 – 34 (20 minutes)

Have a volunteer(s) read the introductory paragraph and Scripture passage, and then discuss the questions that follow.

For thirty years, Jesus seemingly took his place quietly in his family and village. When he began to publicly "teach with authority," drive out demons, heal the sick, clash with religious authorities, and gather his own disciples, the pressures against him intensified. Read Mark 3:20 – 22, 31 – 34:

> [20] Then Jesus entered a house, and again a crowd gathered, so that he and his disciples were not even able to eat. [21] When his family heard about this, they went to take charge of him, for they said, "He is out of his mind."
>
> [22] And the teachers of the law who came down from Jerusalem said, "He is possessed by Beelzebul! By the prince of demons he is driving out demons."
>
> [31] Then Jesus' mother and brothers arrived. Standing outside, they sent someone in to call him. [32] A crowd was sitting around him, and they told him, "Your mother and brothers are outside looking for you."
>
> [33] "Who are my mother and my brothers?" he asked.
>
> [34] Then he looked at those seated in a circle around him and said, "Here are my mother and my brothers!"

3. Place yourself within the crowd in verses 20 – 22. Describe the atmosphere. What do you see, hear, and feel?

4. Now put yourself in Jesus' shoes. Describe the pressure you would be feeling from:

   • Your family

- The religious authorities

5. What self-doubt might you have experienced if you were Jesus?

6. When you take steps to follow God's path for your life and people criticize you or express their disapproval, how do you respond?

SMALL GROUP: Application (17 minutes)

Form groups of three or four to complete this application section. Begin by taking turns to read the introductory paragraphs; then answer questions 7–9 on your own before together sharing your responses (question 10). Afterward, reconvene the large group and answer question 11.

The goal of *The Emotionally Healthy Woman* is to provide you with a fresh vision for transformation in Christ, to offer you a few powerful principles, and to help you think through some commonly accepted ways of approaching life that are not part of the kingdom of God.

Here is a summary of the eight "quits" we have studied together:

- **Quit Being Afraid of What Others Think**
  Anchor your sense of "okayness" in the love of God. Quit relying on the approval of others for your sense of self-worth.

- **Quit Lying**
  Live truly free in unrelenting honesty with yourself, God, and others. Quit pretending everything is fine when it is not.

- **Quit Dying to the Wrong Things**
  Receive the many gifts God has provided for you that nurture and delight your soul. Quit dying to those things that bring you life.

- **Quit Denying Anger, Sadness, and Fear**
  Embrace your God-given humanity by paying attention to your "difficult" emotions and discerning how God wants to come to you through them. Quit ignoring your feelings.

- **Quit Blaming**
  Take responsibility for your own life and happiness. Quit giving away your God-given personal freedom and power.

- **Quit Overfunctioning**
  Don't do for others what they could and should be doing for themselves. Quit trying to control people and situations.

- **Quit Faulty Thinking**
  Choose to live in reality and truth rather than with distorted thinking. Quit making assumptions that will leave you powerless and in unnecessary pain.

- **Quit Living Someone Else's Life**
  Take up the challenge of living your God-given, unique, unrepeatable life and destiny. Quit allowing others to pressure you into trying to be someone God didn't design you to be.

7. As you reflect on the above list, which "quit" impacted you the most? Why?

8. Which "quit" have you found the most difficult to do? Why?

9. In light of your responses to the previous two questions, what is one step God might be calling you to take?

10. In your small group, each briefly share some of your responses to questions 7 – 9.

LARGE GROUP: Moving Forward (20 minutes)

11. Reconvene the large group and share your answers to the following question: What is one hope or dream you have as you move forward and implement these "quits" into your formation as a follower of Christ?

VIDEO: Frequently Asked Questions (5 minutes)

Watch the Frequently Asked Questions video segment for Session 8. The questions are repeated below, should you want to revisit them later on your own or with a friend or other group member. There is also some space provided for note-taking.

- A lot of what you are teaching us has to do with reflection, prayer, and inward listening. Why does God make it so difficult? Why doesn't he just clearly tell us what it means to quit living someone else's life — like he did with Moses?

- I have spent most of my life fulfilling other people's expectations of me. It is hard for me to imagine getting as free as you say I can. I am overwhelmed by what is before me and all of the things I will need to do in order to live as an emotionally healthy woman. Can you give me a few more pointers?

- What next steps should we take now that we have finished this study?

NOTES

Personal Reflection (2 minutes)

Take one minute to still your mind and heart before the Lord and respond to the following question:

> *What is one thing you learned about God, yourself, or others during this session? Write it down.*

Spend one minute answering the following question:

> *What is one step you can take to begin truly living your unique, God-given life today? Write it down.*

Closing Prayer (1 minute)

Use the following prayer or briefly offer your own closing prayer.

Abba, Father, help us to slow down in order to discover our "sealed orders" from you. Enable us to be attuned to your voice day by day. Fill us with the Holy Spirit so that we can live courageously and quit all those things that do not belong to your kingdom. In Jesus' name, amen.

Leader's Guide

General Guidelines

1. Be sure to preview both video segments (main teaching and Frequently Asked Questions) and read the related workbook content before each session. Becoming familiar with the material and instructions will allow you to comfortably lead your group. You will also want to read the corresponding chapter(s) in *The Emotionally Healthy Woman* book before each session.

2. Have copies of this workbook and *The Emotionally Healthy Woman* book available for each participant to purchase at the first two sessions. Make scholarships available, if possible, for those who need financial assistance. Though a person can participate in the group without reading the book, reading the recommended chapter prior to the session tends to make for a deeper transformational impact — and thus is highly recommended.

3. Each session will require 80 – 90 minutes to complete. (The first session, however, takes 95 minutes, as the video includes Geri's story and an overall introduction.) Although the nature of this material lends itself to lengthy sharing, we encourage you to follow the suggested time limits outlined in the workbook. And respect everyone by beginning and ending on time.

4. Set up the meeting room in a way that will comfortably seat all participants, preferably in a circle so that everyone can see each other. Arrive at least 15 minutes ahead of time to test your video player to be sure that it is working properly and to greet group members individually as they come in.

5. To kick off each meeting, read aloud the Introduction found at the beginning of that session of the study guide.

6. Whenever the entire group is asked to break into groups of two to four (mostly in the Application sections), identify a timekeeper for each group so that each person has sufficient time to share. Be sure to mention to your group that everyone always has the choice to share or not share. We invite; we don't pressure. If your group is larger than eight to ten people, you may want to split into smaller groups for some of the other group-sharing exercises as well.

7. At the end of each Application section, there is often an invitation to pray for one another. Several factors will impact how you integrate prayer into the group at this juncture and at the end of the session: the depth and extent of what people are sharing, the time remaining, the level of safety in the group, people's willingness and ability to pray in a larger group, and, most importantly, what the Holy Spirit is doing. You may sometimes find that it is more appropriate for you yourself to close the group in prayer rather than having different people pray aloud.

8. Allow time for group members to complete the Personal Reflection section near the close of each session. This section provides time for people to pause and pay attention to how God is speaking to them specifically and uniquely.

9. When appropriate, it will be helpful if you lead by example — being vulnerable and open with life examples from your own journey.

10. Remember, we are only experts on *our own* journey. Respect where each woman is in her personal journey with Christ. The Holy Spirit will prompt and lead each person differently and at different paces through this material. Remember that people change slowly — and that includes you!

11. *The Emotionally Healthy Woman* is about spiritual formation in Christ; it is not a substitute for counseling. Be aware that there may be people whose needs go beyond the scope of this group. Consider referring those people to counselors and professionals with special expertise. *The Emotionally Healthy Woman* course is not designed to meet in-depth needs.

12. Pray for each member of your group between sessions. Ask that God will enable each woman to grasp the key biblical truths being presented and begin practicing them in her life for personal transformation.

13. A fuller, more developed theology for integrating the missing components of emotionally healthy spirituality can be found in *The Emotionally Healthy Church* and *Emotionally Healthy Spirituality*.

14. Pete and Geri preached a sermon series called "I Quit!" that was based on the themes outlined in this workbook. Except for sessions 6 and 8, each sermon is based on the Bible passages used in this study guide. These messages can be found on the Emotionally Healthy website.

15. Consider having each member of your group take the Inventory on Emotional/Spiritual Maturity, a simple but excellent diagnostic tool for assessing spiritual/emotional health. It is available through the Emotionally Healthy Spirituality mobile app, downloadable from iTunes®. The inventory also can be found in chapter 4 of *The Emotionally Healthy Church*.

Specific Guidelines for Each Session

SESSION 1: *Quit Being Afraid of What Others Think*

In addition to the general guidelines, here are some other helpful items to note by section:

Before the Session

- Read chapter 1 of *The Emotionally Healthy Woman* book.

Introduction/Getting Connected

- This session lasts 95 minutes, as the video includes Geri's story, the overall themes for the next eight weeks, and the introduction to this first session. Let people know this in advance.
- Briefly review the dates and times the group will be meeting.
- Explain your role as facilitator for the group. Let your group know that you won't be lecturing but learning together with them.
- Be sure to read the "Suggested Guidelines for the Group."

- For at least the first session or two, read instructions aloud as indicated in the workbook in order to keep the group moving at the suggested pace.

Bible Study

- *(Question 7)* As a result of Aaron's fears, the whole nation was almost wiped out by God and God's plan for these people was almost derailed. God sent a plague that killed 3,000 people. There was a great deal of pain and confusion. Moreover, Aaron himself was diminished when he went against his better judgment. Some great examples of being afraid of what other people think are given on pages 32 – 34 of *The Emotionally Healthy Woman*.

Application

- By adulthood, we have accumulated millions of messages, both spoken and unspoken, from our families and cultures. These messages tell us what we should do, be, think, and feel in order to be loved and accepted. In the same way, it will be a process for us to rewire our brains to see ourselves as God does.

Frequently Asked Questions

- To cultivate a life more grounded in the love of God, recommend reading chapter 8, "Discover the Rhythms of the Daily Office and Sabbath," in *Emotionally Healthy Spirituality* and *Emotionally Healthy Spirituality Day by Day*.

SESSION 2: *Quit Lying*

In addition to the general guidelines, here are some other helpful items to note by section:

Before the Session

- Read chapter 2 of *The Emotionally Healthy Woman* book.

Getting Connected

- You may want to read the "Suggested Guidelines for the Group" again.
- You may want to read instructions aloud as indicated in the

workbook, or when appropriate, in order to keep the group moving at the suggested pace.

Bible Study

- *(Question 6, part 2)* It may help if you think of specific examples. Think of their ability to love, lack of connectedness, superficiality, lack of life-change, or openness to God.

Frequently Asked Questions

- Geri and Pete will demonstrate being truthful incorrectly (pre-*Emotionally Healthy Woman*) and correctly (post-*Emotionally Healthy Woman*).
- It can be uncomfortable for some of us to speak respectfully, honestly, and clearly — especially if we have been doing it poorly for many years. Remind people that feeling uncomfortable is often a great indication that we are growing and changing. You may also want to refer group members to *The Emotionally Healthy Skills 2.0* curriculum to learn additional tools for relating maturely to others, themselves, and to God.

SESSION 3: *Quit Dying to the Wrong Things*

In addition to the general guidelines, here are some other helpful items to note by section:

Before the Session

- Read chapter 3 of *The Emotionally Healthy Woman* book.

Bible Study

- *(Question 3)* God surveyed his creation with great joy. He recognized "it is good" six times, climaxing with a seventh "very good" in verse 31. God beamed with delight, savoring creation like an artist saying, "What I have done is beautiful. This is spectacular!"
- *(Question 5)* As leader, it is important for you to bring a balance of biblical truth to this discussion. Scripture teaches that human beings are both good (Genesis 1) *and* that we are sinners (Genesis 3). This is

a paradox of biblical theology — an apparent contradiction of truths. We see other such paradoxes in Scripture. For example:

– When you lose your life, you find it.
– The last shall be first.
– Death brings life.
– The more you increase your knowledge, the more you realize how little you know.
– To see the light, you must descend into the darkness.
– We hear in silence.

This subject will be more fully addressed at the end of the Frequently Asked Questions video.

SESSION 4: *Quit Denying Anger, Sadness, and Fear*

In addition to the general guidelines, here are some other helpful items to note by section:

Before the Session

• Read chapter 4 of *The Emotionally Healthy Woman* book.

Bible Study

• *(Question 3)* Notice the picture of bulls, roaring lions hungry for supper, and dogs sniffing for something to eat (Psalm 22:12 – 13). They point to the strength and cruelty of David's enemies. By the end of Psalm 22 (vv. 22 – 31), however, David affirmed that God is the Lord God Almighty. And he committed himself to praising God and fulfilling the vows he had made.

• *(Question 4)* Two-thirds of the Psalms are laments or complaints. Jesus, our Lord and Savior, was a man of sorrows, familiar with pain (Isaiah 53:3). Jesus even quoted Psalm 22:1 from the cross. The ancient Hebrews physically expressed their laments by tearing their clothes and wearing sackcloth and ashes. Jesus himself offered up prayer and petitions with loud cries and tears (Hebrews 5:7). God grieved about the state of humanity during Noah's time (Genesis 6). After the fall of Jerusalem, Jeremiah wrote an entire biblical book called Lamentations. This is in sharp contrast with Western culture today, which so often denies and avoids the difficulties and losses of life.

Application

- *(Questions 7 – 8)* You as a facilitator will want to prepare a personal example, if possible. If you don't have any of your own, use Geri's from *The Emotionally Healthy Woman* book.

SESSION 5: *Quit Blaming*

In addition to the general guidelines, here are some other helpful items to note by section:

Before the Session

- Read chapter 5 of *The Emotionally Healthy Woman* book. In particular, be sure to familiarize yourself with the Personal Freedom Toolkit (pages 121 – 140) so that you will be able to summarize it during the session.

Growing Connected

- *(Question 1)* To kick off this section, be prepared to share a brief example or two from your own life.

Bible Study

- *(Question 4)* Be sure to note that neither Adam nor Eve took responsibility for their choices. Adam blamed Eve. Eve blamed the serpent. Blaming is often a behavior we use to protect or defend ourselves from taking responsibility for our choices.

- *(Questions 5 – 6)* Blaming, sad to say, has always been with us — in every generation, culture, and nation. Satan himself is described in Revelation 12:10 as one who accuses and blames day and night! Encourage the group to reflect on the unique nuances of blaming that they are familiar with from their family members, ethnic group, race, and culture.

  There is a difference between self-confronting and self-blaming. Self-confronting leads to growth; self-blaming leads to condemnation. This also often goes back to our families of origin and messages that were projected onto us. Note that perfectionism is another source of blaming. The demand for a "perfect world" inevitably leads to blaming.

Application

- Be prepared to summarize the different tools before, or during, the discussion. Be sure to leave the full time suggested for this section, as it drives home the application for the entire session.

SESSION 6: *Quit Overfunctioning*

Before the Session

- Read chapter 6 of *The Emotionally Healthy Woman* book. Pay special attention to the section on the deadly consequences of overfunctioning (pages 147 – 158).

Starters

- *(Question 3)* You may need to provide some examples from chapter 6, "Quit Overfunctioning," in *The Emotionally Healthy Woman*. This may also help give a practical picture for those in the group still struggling to understand the concept. Remember, overfunctioning is doing for others what they could and should be doing for themselves.

Bible Study

- *(Question 4)* Martha is angry and resentful — especially at her sister Mary, who sits enjoying the company of Jesus. Martha is too distracted and irritated to enjoy Jesus herself.

- *(Question 6)* Martha could have asked for help, simplified the menu, taken responsibility for her choices, clarified her expectations, or remembered that hospitality is not an end in itself but simply a means to the "one thing essential" (expressing love to God and others).

Application

- Be prepared to summarize the section on the deadly consequences of overfunctioning described in chapter 6 of *The Emotionally Healthy Woman*.

- *(Question 10)* Here are some sample "Remedies." Group members may come up with others.
  - I can ask for help because I too have needs.
  - I don't always need to have things my way because I sometimes get it wrong.
  - I don't always need to be in control because I am not God, and others need the opportunity to take the lead.
  - I can let things go because God is in control and on the throne ruling the universe.
  - My way is not always the best way because God makes people different, and he often has different journeys for other people.
  - I don't have to do everything myself because God is the One who acts on my behalf. Moreover, God invites me to be a receiver as well as a giver.

SESSION 7: *Quit Faulty Thinking*

Before the Session

- Read chapter 7 of *The Emotionally Healthy Woman* book. Pay special attention to the section on the three types of faulty thinking (pages 171 – 181).

Growing Connected

- *(Question 1)* It will be helpful for you to have some personal examples to prompt others in the group to share.

Bible Study

- Elijah was in great emotional pain and not thinking clearly. God intervened by personally coming to him and gently meeting his most pressing need for food and sleep, thus strengthening Elijah for the next steps he would need to take. Elijah was then able to see and hear God in a fresh way (v. 11). Finally, God informed Elijah that he was not alone at all; seven thousand persons faithful to the God of Israel also remained (v. 18).

Application

- Be able to summarize the three types of faulty thinking described in chapter 7 of *The Emotionally Healthy Woman*.
- *(Question 7)* Here are some sample answers to the empty boxes:
  - *My friend never responded to my email:* I shouldn't assume that I'm not important to her. It may be that she never received my email. It is possible she forgot to reply. It may be that she didn't know I was expecting a reply right away.
  - *I'll never be in a healthy dating relationship:* I can learn the skills and find the help needed for a successful dating relationship. My past does not have to be my future.
  - *My coworker is a terrible employee:* I shouldn't focus solely on the negative. My coworker is really insightful and skilled in some areas, and not well-suited for this job in other areas.

SESSION 8: *Quit Living Someone Else's Life*

Before the Session

- Read chapter 8 of *The Emotionally Healthy Woman* book.

Growing Connected

- *(Question 1)* This section is only given four minutes intentionally. Its purpose is brief connection. The rest of the session will return to this theme. Moreover, it is essential that you leave sufficient time for the Application and Moving Forward sections in this final meeting.

Bible Study

- Remember, Jesus "has been tempted in every way, just as we are" (Hebrews 4:15).
- *(Question 4)* In the ancient world, it was extremely important to honor one's mother and father. Jesus demonstrated that value, even when he was hanging on the cross. Yet Jesus was direct and clear in calling people to a first loyalty to himself over their biological families, saying, "Anyone who loves their father or mother more than me is not worthy of me" (Matthew 10:37). For a fuller exploration of this

theme, see chapter 5, "Going Back to Go Forward," in *Emotionally Healthy Spirituality*.

Moving Forward

- Be sure to leave sufficient time for question 11, giving group members an opportunity to share their future hopes and dreams with one another.

The Emotionally Healthy Christian

The following inventory is adapted from the *Emotionally Healthy Skills 2.0 Workbook* (page 99):

- I am deeply convinced that I am loved by Christ, and as a result, I don't inappropriately borrow that love from others.
- I love my neighbor as I love myself — embracing my singleness as I bond with others, or in marriage, giving first priority to my spouse and children.
- I am able to detach from my family of origin and function as an inner-directed, separate adult.
- I am deeply in tune with my own emotions and feelings.
- I am able to listen with empathy without having to fix, change, or save others.
- I can speak clearly, honestly, and respectfully on my own behalf.
- I can express my anger, hurt, or fear without blaming, appeasing, or holding grudges.
- Through self-respect and self-care, I value my own dignity as a human being made in God's image.
- I walk in community while respecting each person's uniqueness.
- I can receive criticism without defensiveness.
- I can state my own beliefs and values without becoming adversarial.
- I live in truth, not pretense, spin, illusions, or exaggerations.
- I embrace my limits as gifts.

- I am able to negotiate, respect, and celebrate the ways I am different from others — and the ways in which they are different from me.
- I am willing to initiate and repair relationships (as much as it is possible) when they have been ruptured.

Notes

1. Thomas Merton, *New Seeds of Contemplation* (New York: New Directions Publishing, reprint ed. 2007; first ed. 1961), n.p.

2. Henri J. M. Nouwen, *The Return of the Prodigal Son: A Story of Homecoming* (New York: Doubleday, 1992), 107.

3. These questions are adapted from the much larger, more complete "Inventory of Emotional/Spiritual Maturity" found in chapter 4 of *The Emotionally Healthy Church* (Zondervan, 2010). It is also available through the Emotionally Healthy Spirituality mobile app, available for download on iTunes®.

4. See *The Emotionally Healthy Woman*, 121 – 140.

5. We also recommend using the skill "Climb the Ladder of Integrity." This is explained and modeled in Session 6 of *Emotionally Healthy Skills 2.0* and can be downloaded from iTunes® as part of the Emotionally Healthy Spirituality app.

6. John Powell, S.J., *Will the Real Me Please Stand Up?: 25 Guidelines for Good Communication* (Allen, Texas: Tabor Publishing, 1985), 39.

The Emotionally Healthy Woman

Eight Things You Have to Quit to Change Your Life

Geri Scazzero with Peter Scazzero

Geri Scazzero knew there was something desperately wrong with her life. She felt like a single parent raising her four young daughters alone. She finally told her husband, "I quit," and left the thriving church he pastored, beginning a journey that transformed her and her marriage for the better.

In *The Emotionally Healthy Woman*, Geri provides you a way out of an inauthentic, superficial spirituality to genuine freedom in Christ. This book is for every woman who thinks, "I can't keep pretending everything is fine!"

The journey to emotional health begins by quitting. Geri quit being afraid of what others think. She quit lying. She quit denying her anger and sadness. She quit living someone else's life. When you quit those things that are damaging to your soul or the souls of others, you are freed up to choose other ways of being and relating that are rooted in love and lead to life.

When you quit for the right reasons, at the right time, and in the right way, you're on the path not only to emotional health, but also to the true purpose of your life.

"QUITTING WILL SET YOU FREE!

Not a typical message heard in the church today, especially among 'nice, Christian women,' but one that has been needed for years! By refusing to cling to a shell of pretension, the true freedom of our new lives in Christ is realized, and Geri shows us how. A fast, informed read, this book breaks down the walls of the false ideals we cling to in and shows us that by quitting these idols, we rediscover God's love. I was supposed to read this book. I needed to read this book. Thank you, Geri."

Kim de Blecourt, Short-term Adventure Specialist with
Food for Orphans and author of *Until We All Come Home:
A Harrowing Journey, a Mother's Courage, a Race to Freedom*

Emotionally Healthy Spirituality

It's Impossible to Be Spiritually Mature, While Remaining Emotionally Immature

Peter Scazzero

Peter Scazzero learned the hard way: you can't be spiritually mature while remaining emotionally immature. Even though he was a pastor of a growing church, he did what most people do:

- avoided conflict in the name of Christianity
- ignored his anger, sadness, and fear
- used God to run from God
- lived without boundaries

Eventually God awakened him to a biblical integration of emotional health, a relationship with Jesus, and the classic practices of contemplative spirituality. It created nothing short of a spiritual revolution, utterly transforming him and his church.

In this bestselling book Scazzero outlines his journey and the signs of emotionally unhealthy spirituality. He then goes on to provide seven biblical, reality-tested ways to break through to the revolutionary life Christ meant for you. "The combination of emotional health and contemplative spirituality," he says, "unleashes the Holy Spirit inside us so that we might experientially know the power of an authentic life in Christ."

Available in stores and online!

For more information on implementing
Emotionally Healthy Spirituality and
Emotionally Healthy Spirituality Day by Day
into your life, small group, or church, go to:

www.emotionallyhealthy.org